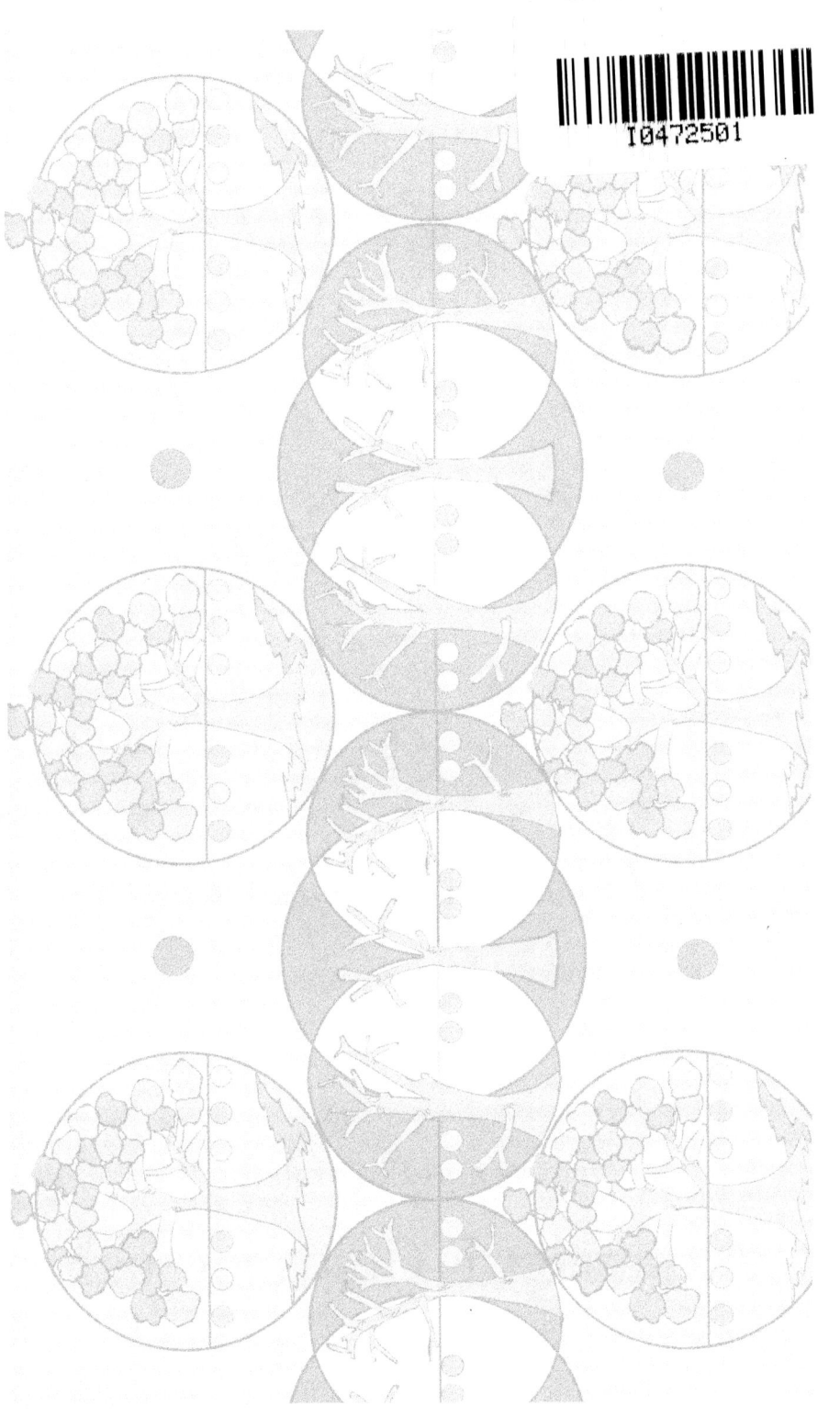

Creativity, Strategy, and Leadership for Entrepreneurs

Written and Illustrated by

Alexander F. Goldsborough

ACKNOWLEDGMENTS

My gratitude to Peter, my son, whose brilliant youth, intellectual curiosity, patience and love was a source of inspiration, bonding and learning.

He is the author of: www.aesopforentrepreneurs.com

To my students, I hope to have successfully helped you develop the mindset and skillset required to successfully launch and operate an entrepreneurial venture. Business is not only a science, but also an art; new ideas and opportunities often come from observing and understanding patterns of behavior, and human needs and wants, that have little changed over time. Ancient wisdom, whether stories, proverbs, or adages, is packed with valuable advice for making better decisions as a leader, thinking out-of-the-box, stimulating divergent thinking, and helping to reframe complex problems entrepreneurs face today.

"History doesn't repeat itself but it often rhymes."
Mark Twain.

The proverbs are taken from the Adagia of Erasmus, a collection of Greek and Latin proverbs, with explanations relating to entrepreneurship written by the author.

The illustrations are by the author. All referenced works are in the public domain.

Other titles by Alexander F. Goldsborough:

Aesop for Entrepreneurs

Aesop for Entrepreneurs, Fables 26-50

www.aesopforentrepreneurs

BUSINESS IS THE
SALT OF LIFE

Everybody is buying and selling, everything's
for sale, everyone's for hire, we learn the art of the
transaction, the deal, the negotiation, the dreamed
of lifestyle, all becomes a matter of doing business.
Entrepreneurs "do" business not because they're
insane or bored, but because they want to build
a better boat to navigate the rivers of their life; to
become a business-person, as a pathway to becoming
financially independent, successful, and rich. The
business becomes the salt of life, becomes the salt
mine, becomes a commodity producing vehicle; it's
a conduit for the creation of value, to distribute the
salt of ideas, solving salty problems requiring spicy
solutions, and helping other people run businesses
to become worth their salt. If the purpose of business
is to become independent, then it isn't to become
salt free; but for the sake of happiness, comfort and
freedom, to produce as much salt as possible, and
dough too.

LONG ABSENT SOON FORGOTTEN

It's important never to drift too far, and always remain present in the customer's life. They are a fickle creature, constantly changing their minds and switching loyalties. They are savvy, and careful about what they buy; and they like to shop around. On the other hand, entrepreneurs strive for maximum brand recognition at minimum cost; advertisement is expensive, and a recurring cost. To have and offer the best of both worlds, entrepreneurs need to be creative, adopt guerrilla marketing tactics, reframing problems in their quest for solutions by thinking "outside-the-box". The going isn't always easy; a learning curve comes at a cost, as mistakes are expensive, and customers impatient. Entrepreneurs must iterate, pivot and fail fast, until they find the business model that best serves their vision and objectives, making sure they're never absent long from their market segment.

THERE IS NO ACCORD WHERE EVERY MAN WOULD BE A LORD

As the company grows, and new employees are hired, it becomes necessary for the entrepreneur to step into the shoes of a leader. Without a leader, a structure, and a hierarchy, it becomes difficult for a growing company to function. The leader defines the corporate culture, the power distance between employees, the degree of collaboration, flatness of hierarchy. There are bound to be problems and conflicts as power struggles can emerge, employees disagreeing and creating disharmony. There can't be too many cooks in the kitchen, at the same time an entrepreneur can't do it all. He doesn't want to become a micro-manager, which can become frustrating for an entrepreneur who's strength is to focus on the big strategic picture. Therefore he must learn to delegate and hire good managers, so he can continue to do what's he's good at. By distributing tasks everyone becomes lord in their area of expertise.

NO LIVING MAN ALL THINGS CAN

When scanning the market for startup ideas, the greatest efforts are poured into identifying a problem and offering a viable solution to customers. Entrepreneurs seek to maximize the chances of making money, while reducing risk of failure to a minimum. Chances of success are better when an entrepreneur tackles one problem at a time. Spending more time on research and testing products by prioritizing their importance to the company's bottom line, image and reputation. Classifying the product portfolio according to potential gains and reduced risks for example, is far more efficient, increasing productivity as employees are less confused and focus on one problem at a time. Cash flow will dictate when the time is right to take on more risks. Proper organization is all about timing, discipline, focus, specialization and owning the solution to the problem being solved.

ALMOST AND VERY NEAR
SAVES MANY A LIFE

The fear of failure is what drives entrepreneurs to work endless long hours. Gravitational forces want to pull them down, forcing them to come crashing down to earth. Only the entrepreneur's hard work, and hiring the right talent, keeps the startup propped up - to face another day, another battle for survival. There are near deaths, as mistakes are inevitable; the trick is to keep the failures small and manageable, never failing completely and remaining alive to face another day. In the early days, running a company it's brutal grunt work, the end seemingly always so near, victory snatched from the jaws of defeat. It's important to manage small mistakes before they lead to complete failures, constantly feeding new opportunities and eliminating threats, regulating the healthy heart beats of the company; almost succeeding is still failure; almost failing can still bring success.

HE THAT'S AFRAID OF LEAVES MUST NOT COME IN A WOOD

There are many aspects of running a company that don't match up to the glamorous idea many have. Making huge profits is arguably the fun part, but that part comes later, at first, he must be ready to spend long hours doing work that might not be all that fun. Those afraid of getting their hands dirty, spending long hours crunching numbers, dealing with difficult customers, unreliable suppliers, constant problems, risks, dangers, the daily struggle - shouldn't embark on the entrepreneurship voyage. There may be a pot of gold lying on the horizon, but the waters to get there are infested with deadly underwater creatures, who, no matter where you run or how fast you run, will hunt you down to make you fail. Success comes from accepting to deal with the parts that are not fun, in order to get to the parts that are.

HE IS NEVER LIKELY TO HAVE A GOOD THING CHEAP THAT IS AFRAID TO ASK THE PRICE

A shy entrepreneur is one with two marks of weakness stamped on their forehead; a polite entrepreneur has one mark. Both cases lead to a failed business. It's perfectly OK to risk offending a supplier who's prices are not aligned with the entrepreneur's business model. Taking a tough position is the nature of negotiation. In many cultures, being polite because they've invited you to dinner to soften you up, doesn't mean they won't gouge you during a negotiation. There's a time for proper dainty manners, and a time dealing with business. In business, to be shy is to be weak - to pretend to be shy is a negotiation tactic. In business, to be overly polite, not wanting to offend is weakness - to use politeness as an instrument to soften up potential clients isn't fair, but it's fair play. It's important for entrepreneurs to think and act strategically.

ADVERSITY MAKES A MAN WISE NOT RICH

With experience, the tolerance for dealing with adversity increases. Gaining experience comes from being exposed to adversity. With greater experience comes greater knowledge, allowing the entrepreneur to take on greater risks. Experience provides knowledge and insight, necessary to create and implement new business strategies, setting the company on the right course, giving it an added edge in the market. To anyone outside this process, the level of adversity, risk and pressure is intolerable, but to the experienced entrepreneur, expert in his niche, everyday is a new normal. Risking nothing, hiding from adversity, makes experience and insight impossible, no edge, no novelty, no ideas, no product or profit. Embracing adversity however, brings the experience and expertise which makes an entrepreneur wise - the greatest of all riches.

ANGER IS SHORT-LIVED
IN A MAN

It's hard enough to succeed as an entrepreneur without adding to the burden. Anger is a destructive emotion which clouds judgment and antagonizes stakeholders. Anger creates stress, and becomes a vicious cycle when a previous bout of anger induces errors, and guilt, which fuel a new cycle of anger, until the company fails. Nobody likes to be shouted at; the role of the entrepreneur is not to be a bully but a mentor, inspiring not alienating. Given that risks of failure are greater than chances to succeed, entrepreneurs need to work on not becoming their own worst enemy. Entrepreneurs must remain focused on building a positive, empowering environment, and substituting for anger the virtuous powers of professionalism and creativity. The only place for anger is as a strategic tool when negotiating a contract for example, as emphasis, to manipulate the opposition, to add pressure to gain an advantage.

A GOOD MAN CANNOT LIVE BY THE AIR

At one point it becomes important for an entrepreneur to move from the stage of brainstorming, planning and forming hypotheses to that of action and implementation. Until that point everything is theory - moving to the next stage makes everything suddenly very real. Subjecting the theory to the real world is testing the validity of hypotheses, the robustness of a plan, the entrepreneurs character. Ideas alone are ethereal, virtual, illusory, dream-like, fun, horsing-around, creative, presumptuous, delusional, hopeful - market forces are real, raw, crude, risky, brutal, expensive, tiring, hard, stressful, intense, disappointing, slow, confusing, fearful, strategic, threatening. Entrepreneurs live between the air and market forces, how the two are combined determines the company's fate especially when times are tough.

ALMOST WAS NEVER HANGED

Sometimes playing it safe can land entrepreneurs into serious trouble, especially if their ideas requires them to be bold and adventurous. Managers are given resources and follow per-established guidelines for reaching set objectives. Entrepreneurs would be so lucky - they need to imagine new goals and create new resources using means they don't have and are difficult to get. There are fewer recipes for entrepreneurs, they make do with the contents of the cupboard to create original recipes they can brand and commercialize as their own. They're prepared to push the envelope, take on far more risk, playing brinkmanship with the hangman's noose. If the strategic choices they made and risks they take can get them into trouble - it's their careful planning, experience and discipline that enable them to toy with the rope and at the last minute, walk away. Nobody said entrepreneurship wasn't risky.

SCALD NOT YOUR LIPS IN ANOTHER MAN'S SOUP

One of the main reasons why entrepreneur's decide to take on the challenges and risks of launching their own startup, is a strong desire for freedom and independence. If they're going to get burned, they prefer it be drinking their own soup, designed and marketed by themselves. When making their own soup they can control and offer just the right temperature to customers. They don't envision themselves selling someone else's soups, they have the confidence to think they can do it better - that's the challenge and goal they've set for themselves; and that's their branding and marketing message: new original homemade recipes, using the best available ingredients, unique tastes and flavors at the right temperature - setting their taste buds free! Entrepreneurship is about freedom and independence - that's the taste both the entrepreneur and customer are after.

NEVER BE ASHAMED TO EAT
YOUR MEAT

If the entrepreneur doesn't care and believe in their product, the customer also won't. Building reputation and authenticity requires the affirmation of belief the service product or process will not only work but surpass expectations. The owner has passion because he cares about the customer. The customer trusts, because the owner cares. This is the best meat in town, the best product and service and we're doing it for you! Evaluating customer needs, the entrepreneur delivers what they need, makes them happy - they deserve the best, nothing less - for that, they're always thankful. Good reputation is a virtuous cycle, the owner cares, so does the customer, so do their friends, so does free publicity, so does the banker, so do the suppliers. Caring feeds the company, feeds the entrepreneur, feeds the customer, feeds the world.

HE LOVES BACON WELL THAT LICKS THE SWINE-STY DOOR

Entrepreneurship is a labor of love, with emphasis on labor. The love is spiritual sustenance that drives the momentum forward, the labor is the tactical moves, the careful planning, the detail, the grunt. The love is the inspiration, the labor is the perspiration, which truly does represent 99% of the effort. It's the love that gets the entrepreneurs past the hardship of licking many sty doors before they reach their happy goal of watching customers eat the top quality bacon they offer. But before the entrepreneur can make his own bacon, it's more about tightening the belt than gorging on it. The memories of all that hard work is what stays with the entrepreneur, who wears such an achievement with honor and pride. Be suspicious of those who claim to be entrepreneurs and yet don't know how to lick a pig-sty door squeaky clean.

THAT WHICH IS GOOD FOR THE BACK IS BAD FOR THE HEAD

There comes a point when hiring new help becomes important for sustained growth. Entrepreneurs like to do it all themselves, thinking nobody else cares like they do. Yet, becoming an effective leader is learning to let go of control, and trust colleagues; lightening the load is key to giving the back some rest and freeing up the mind. A startup can literally consume the entrepreneur, so focused is he on his work, deep in the zone - this can cause burnout. As key resource, hiring new talent frees-up the entrepreneur to focus on what he does best - create, plan, organize, strategize, network, raise capital, manage stakeholders, attract new customers, build brand, launch new advertising campaigns, communicate, back new products, troubleshoot, pivot, iterate, hire, fire. All matters of the head.

WHERE BAD'S THE BEST, NOTHING MUST BE THE CHOICE

Entrepreneur's who have trouble making decisions, and saying no to bad choices ought to consider another line of business. Sometimes doing nothing is better than doing the wrong thing. When running a company everyday is truly a new day, and the wrong choice can bring about the complete destruction of the company. Success often comes not necessarily from making the best choices, but from eliminating the worse decisions. When all the worse choices have been eliminated, good decisions stand a better chance of succeeding. Entrepreneur's get themselves into trouble because they believe they must always make a choice, even when all the possible choices are the worse. It's important to learn how to make decisions based on sound choices; and develop the discipline to create and discover better choices, which helps make better decisions.

A BAD BUSH IS BETTER THAN THE OPEN FIELD

Companies have their secrets, information they'd prefer rivals and even stakeholders not to know regarding: market share, profitability, supply chain, market segments, marketing research and more. The information they do share should be strategically intended and calculated - contributing towards building the image and reputation of the company, or its corporate culture, obtaining for great customer feedback, approval from important stakeholders. Strategic can mean making use of disinformation to disorient, deflect propaganda put out to trick and mislead rivals. Entrepreneurs must learn about the type of terrain on which they operate, fight guerrilla style if required: ambush, skirmish and laying traps; using misdirection forcing rivals to make mistakes. In the competitive environment, each type of terrain has advantages and disadvantages, its knowledge is fundamental to making accurate strategic and tactical decisions.

WHEN MISERY IS HIGHEST
PROFIT IS LOWEST

Regardless of how much entrepreneurs would like everyday to be filled with success, reality is more sobering. Small failures are not the end of the world, but the experience is unnerving for personality types expecting instant gratification. These are tests, and part of success is overcoming these obstacles, and defeating inner emotional dragons. Negative thinking creates a vicious cycle, undermining the entrepreneurs self-belief and self confidence. Believing that everything is terrible, becoming easily discouraged, despairing at the slightest sign of adversity, adds to the risks of failure. Remaining level-headed contributes to surviving the setbacks, and overcoming the obstacles. Negative energy is contagious, customers want to feel inspired, positive and happy from their purchase, not discouraged, negative and unhappy. From that type of energy they run.

A BALD HEAD IS
SOON SHAVEN

It's easy to confuse and complicate; it takes extreme discipline to simplify, crystallize, cut to the essential. Although hard work at first, moving up the learning curve, and thinking efficiently comes from practice. Before making a decision, the entrepreneur must learn to reflect, and make choices that have the best risk/reward, cost/benefit. Experience and confidence help make better decisions. Knowing when it's better to carry out the job in-house or outsource to a third party is about being more efficient, simplifying the process. Such a decision helps entrepreneurs better run their company without overburdening themselves with expensive resources. Efficiency gains help the company remain ahead of the competition, a bald head is far more efficient to manage, as long as the entrepreneur doesn't complicate everything by forgetting to shave.

A GOOD FACE NEEDS NO BAND; AND A BAD ONE DESERVES NONE

Creating a positive brand image is helpful to an entrepreneur trying to establish credibility and authenticity in an crowded and competitive marketplace. Much free publicity can be had if a startup has a story people want to hear about; it needs no introduction, it already has a good reputation. Designing an effective communication strategy becomes an important strategic element in articulating the companies vision, mission and objectives. Not-for-profit companies don't need a band to announce their intentions, their moral and ethical message provides them with enough credible face value. A bad reputation needs a louder band to distract and deflect, and cover up the sound of jeering and heckling coming from the crowd. An entrepreneur should always work hard to maintain authenticity, credibility and a positive brand image. As soon as the entrepreneur hears the sound of a band, it's time to revisit the brand image.

MORE WORDS THAN ONE
GO TO A BARGAIN

Using discounts to promote products is a great way to bring attention to a company, if it's done well. Everybody loves a bargain, and in a connected world, it's a lot easier to communicate using social media. Word-of-mouth marketing, or buzz marketing, is a powerful form of free advertising, as customers share a good bargain with each other. Adding visuals to a marketing campaign helps energize the message, as images are worth a thousand words, reinforcing the image and brand identify. Researching the target market segment helps align product to market needs. Incorrect positioning of a bargain is a waste of valuable resources; offering discounts to bait and switch can alienate customers; too many discounts can hurt the bottom line. Using a bargain to pull in customers is fair play, but wrongly done, buzz marketing will not lift but sink the company.

THE GREATEST BARKERS
BITE NOT SOREST

For entrepreneurs starting out, the bite of the customers is the most feared of all. The greatest threat isn't the loud customers, but the quiet one's who say nothing but react by spending nothing too. Favorable online feedback can go viral; the bite of criticism moves fast and can hurt, but isn't necessarily fatal. It is possible to recover from a bad reputation, but it takes dedication, time and great professionalism. Everybody likes a comeback story, and if the entrepreneur is able to win back trust then the biggest barkers, who are the customers, will often give a second chance, and the quiet one's will follow the court of public opinion. Regaining trust is a humbling experience, and humility is a powerful way of building trust. Entrepreneurs must learn to love the loudness of its customers, whose feedback may be the most constructive, learning to profit from it, by listening and nipping problems in the bud before they goes viral, before he hears the bark.

A GOOD BARGAIN IS
A PICK PURSE

Repeat business is a powerful way of generating profit over time. Building reputation off of having great bargains and low prices is an effective way to build a loyal following. However bargains are a double-edged sword for startups. On the one hand customers are pulled in by the allure of a good bargain, and then cross-sold other products for nice profits; on the other customers get used to low prices and when they don't get more they move on to rivals. Finding the balance between the two is important. Good bargains create favorable buzz marketing, but may attract the kind of customer who only shops when there's a bargain. If entrepreneur wants to offer value, it shouldn't be at the expense of his sustainability; he must protect his profit margin and cash flow. However, it's different if his core value proposition is to always offer bargains, and he organizes his supply chain to allow this, then he becomes the pick-purser.

'TIS A HARD BATTLE THAT NONE ESCAPES

Given all the moving parts, entrepreneurship is not the easiest of challenges, which is why it's important to have a strategy. Without one, it's easy to quickly get sucked into the undercurrents and lose control of the battle. Even if the entrepreneur isn't looking for trouble, the murky waters will come to him. A good strategy helps manage the day to day handling of the endless tasks, countless micro decisions aimed at precision positioning in the market. Mistakes cause a lot of lost energy and poor use of resources, a good plan helps mitigate the risk of all kinds of errors: from internal to external threats; supplies dropping the ball; cash crunches; customer complaints, key talent poached by rivals. It's impossible to survive the turbulence of the deep waters of business without a sound strategy, without which success becomes harder than necessary.

EVERY BEAN HAS ITS BLACK

Running a business, even the simplest, is a humbling experience. Determining what it takes to succeed is the subject of many books on entrepreneurship, out to identify the secret to success, the magical formula, the secret recipe for turning lead into gold. At best, theories are elegant, all the pieces of the puzzle seemingly identified, mapped out - but when put into practice don't seem to fit anymore. Theory must be put into practice, where the entrepreneur learns by doing what isn't written in the books, can't be written down; each experience is uniquely different. Entrepreneurship cannot be learned in class, or rigidly memorized. The answers to success are not to be found in a multiple choice questionnaire, nor in case studies, or elegant formulas; but in the trenches, learning to ask the right questions, analyzing the markets correctly. What was true yesterday no longer applies today, theory is the past, practice the today.

SELL NOT THE BEAR'S SKIN BEFORE YOU HAVE CAUGHT HIM

Although an idea might be a multi-million dollar idea, it doesn't mean the entrepreneur will succeed in obtaining a multi-million; he may also lose a million dollars. There are too many examples of seemingly valueless ideas becoming game changers, disrupting consumer behavior and the assumptions of legions of experts. Yet the allure of future profits is seductive and many entrepreneurs lose touch with reality; embarking on high stakes, massive projects hoping to make it big fast. Before the millions can be brought to the bank, there are many steps, each as perilous as the next. If getting past the bear promises to deliver the millions, then the problem is getting past the bear - it's best to have a solid plan, be down-to-earth, because the bear's for real. Many false illusions have been diced-up by the infernal bear's claws - digging deep into the ego, ripping into emotional delusions and false assumptions.

EVERY ASS THINKS HIMSELF WORTHY TO STAND WITH THE KING'S HORSES

If an entrepreneur can handle being an ass first, he'll better handle being a first class horse. Aspiring to being a horse is one thing, but getting ahead of themselves is quite another. This has nothing to do with not believing in yourself, that's a separate issue of managing emotional mindset. When approaching market forces being an ass has its advantages, if anything because it has less to lose. Asses are more cautious and willing to learn. Market forces are pitiless, have no feelings, and will go out of their way to punish asses who think they're horses. Being an ass isn't easy or fun, but it's a rite of passage, and a necessary stage for learning the ropes. A good horse first learns to be a good ass; only the best asses get to be the king's horses; cutting corners carries its risks. Skill development is a process which takes time and goes through stages - it doesn't happen overnight no matter what the ego yearns for.

AN ASS WAS NEVER CUT OUT FOR A LAPDOG

By specializing, the entrepreneur spends time becoming an expert in his field, rather than a jack-of-all-trade and master of none. When customers understand what the entrepreneur stands for, they know whom to turn to in time of need. The entrepreneur's job is to create that connection placing his name brand between problem and solution. It's more difficult with a jack-of-all-trade, who may do many things, but none of them well; people want a good price, but they also want the best quality. Switching to being a lap dog when a reputation has been built on being an ass doesn't help the customer not the bottom line. Success is aided by being focused, maintaining a consistent brand message, not trying to please all the people all of the time, being everything to everyone, and running risk of becoming nothing to nobody.

HE MUST HAVE IRON NAILS THAT SCRATCHES A BEAR

Searching for the best ideas sometimes requires looking in places others wouldn't dare go; or connecting dots others wouldn't consider; or making assumptions regarding consumer tastes and needs at which others would laugh. Yet, many great entrepreneurial successes are carried out by those for whom only the iron nails of boldness and creativity are the best defense against poking the bear of the competitive market. The market plays dirty, using only rusty iron nails to dance. The entrepreneur and the market dance by holding each other with a firm grip. Losing his grip, the entrepreneur wouldn't last long; he must dig in by bing creative, unconventional and lead the dance. Success must be earned, it isn't given, each scratch a badge rewarding courage, daring, creativity, unconventional thinking, balanced mindset. This is the nature of the bear dance.

A MAN MAY BEAR 'TILL HIS BACK BREAKS

If the entrepreneur doesn't learn to say no, she soon finds herself knee deep in confusion as ideas both good and bad swarm about her and never crystallize into a clear and precise path forward. A strategy that is full on contradictions and ambiguities isn't a strategy but a formula for failure. When starting out at first, the back is weak, and can easily break. Learning to say no helps to learn how to say yes and make the right choices; learning how to fail helps learn to succeed; learning to be efficient helps make the back strong enough to handle the heavy loads. Learning not to promise the world, and instead focus on one core market segment at a time takes discipline; whereas, saying yes to a thousand customers, when doing so is impossible, is a formula for burnout and eventual bankruptcy. Better to capture a small share at first, than no share at all, and focus on strengthening the back over time.

HE'LL BEAR IT AWAY IF IT NOT BE TOO HOT OR TOO HEAVY

Entrepreneurs create and innovate, it's what defines them and differentiates them from others involved in business. They take on the challenges and bear the risks, but are not foolhardy. They are neither merchants buying and selling, nor managers organizing existing resources with clear objectives guiding them forward. Entrepreneurs are at first unclear of the destination, focused on testing their hypotheses for which there exists no recipe to follow, not clearly lit path; they will manage their environment to make risk manageable. Where the entrepreneur walks and looks, ideas come to life; he is the inventor and the creator, the builder, the architect. He's vulnerable to theft and pirating, but he protects his ideas by registering a patent, a copyright, a trademark, and uses the law to regulate the temperature of risks, such that they neither scald nor freeze either his motivations or creative imagination.

ALL THAT ARE IN BED MUST NOT HAVE QUIET REST

Little by little what starts out as a few hours a week, soon turns into 50, 60, 70+ working hours per week. Respecting the boundaries between professional and private life is possibly the hardest skill an entrepreneur must learn. Working less hours but efficiently, is better than more hours in a state of burnout. It's not about the quantity of work, but its quality; an entrepreneur must have periods of quiet rest. Quality of life is about finding that work/life balance. A tired, frustrated, stressed, burned-out entrepreneur is one who makes mistakes, forgets, sleeps badly, gets snappy with customers and suppliers, grows angry and loses motivation. Maintaining high motivation at all times is critical. When sleeping, the entrepreneur must sleep on both ears. There's a time for the quiet of rest; and a time for loudness of work.

WHERE BEES ARE, THERE IS HONEY

There are more ideas than there are entrepreneurs, yet finding a good idea is not easy. As part of their quest for success and wealth creation, entrepreneurs work hard to identify, position and differentiate themselves from others in the market. They target a particular segment of the market, where consumer tastes are aligned with the value proposition they offer. There's no point in selling a product into a non-existent market. Often, the path of least resistance is following the trend and selling into a market where the bees fly. Riding the wave of a niche market is a powerful strategy when starting out, taking care to add value to the new product innovation, identifying a gap and a need not being satisfied. Innovation can include offering a product which taps into previously unidentified latent demand, and a whole new market is created. Once the trend identified or created, it's time to harvest.

BEGGARS MUST BE
NO CHOOSERS

The hardest part of launching a startup is getting enough traction to get to the break-even point as quickly as possible. Dealing with money can confuse a lot of novice entrepreneurs; yet it's a skill which can't be ignored and must be mastered. Writing a business plan proposing a hypothesis for possible future performance, modeling future earnings and hoped for outcomes; preparing financial statements, crunching the numbers as part of the day-to-day reality of running the business. Learning to manage cash-flow is vital to long term sustainability, and allows the entrepreneur to re-invest and eventually scale the company. With everything to lose, and little market power, not exaggerating future performance by making unrealistic financial projections, helps provide the entrepreneur with more flexibility and possible choices for dealing with future constraints, obstacles and threats, giving them more control over their destiny.

IT IS BETTER TO BE A BEGGAR THAN A FOOL

An entrepreneur is a humble servant to the customer; it isn't he who does the customer a favor, it's the other way around. Only a fool bent on failure would disagree. It is better to be a beggar, offering a quality service, competently and with humility, working hard to make the customer happy, than to think the customer's only purpose is to bring in the money. Good salesmanship is not convincing the customer to hand over their money; it's about creating a rapport and relationship to make the customer want to come back, want to talk about their experience with their friends and family, and want to part with their hard-earned money. It's all about rapport, trust, building relationships, giving respect. First comes the trust, then comes the money; better to be a humble, thankful beggar, than an annoying braggart and a fool.

A GOOD BEGINNING MAKES A GOOD ENDING

Failing to plan is planning to fail. Given the uncertainties and ambiguities of the market, it's always a good idea for entrepreneurs to spend extra time preparing their business model. It's impossible to predict the future, but it is possible to build a model that helps mitigate against unexpected occurrences, reduce risk and potential threats. Rushing to spend money on marketing, advertising, and building up inventory without having carefully tested the market is a dangerous proposition. A good beginning starts with testing, and putting in place a solid foundation on which to grow the company. Testing hypotheses, organizing focus groups, always asking questions and investigating assumptions is part of preparation. Obtaining and analyzing feedback in the early stages, helps visualize the market, and map out future directions, to reduce error and maximize the chances of success. Sloppy initial preparation can comes back to haunt the entrepreneur.

WELL BEGUN IS HALF DONE

Many of the skills required by entrepreneurs to successfully manage a company, are not necessarily taught in business school. The best business school is not in the classroom, but out in the actual market, where crucial skills are learned: common sense, learning how to prioritize, communication skills, soft skills, being organized. Many of these skills can't be learned out of a book but must be experienced. Business schools offer a structure and a learning framework - it's a start, albeit an expensive one, to learn about finance, accounting, strategy, leadership, marketing, corporate communications and the usual business school fare. What isn't learned are the shades of gray, the nuances, the rules of thumb, and tricks of the trade, which can actually make all the difference. Getting an education is a good start, the job of learning to be an effective entrepreneur is only half done, if that.

BELIEVE WELL AND HAVE WELL

It's precisely when times get tough that entrepreneurs have to dig deep inside themselves and find the courage and discipline to pivot the company into the right direction. Believing in success, in the mission and the vision is half the battle. Starting a company is like playing a game, you win some and you lose some, the key to success is winning more than losing. Maintaining a strong mindset is critical to this process. Believing in success helps get over the negative bumps n the road, giving up is the easy way out, the immature way out. The critical thinking, rational mind doesn't cave in to emotions, instead it returns to the drawing board and considers the next strategic move. Self-improvement, confidence and efficacy is part of believing in victory; giving up is cheating oneself of believing in success; entrepreneur's can't afford to be their own worst enemy - that's the work of the competitors.

THE BELLY HATH NO EARS

There is nothing more dangerous than an entrepreneur with his back to the wall. As business is both a science and an art, entrepreneurs will create, innovate, and pivot their way out of a corner. Throwing punches with new ideas; kicking with speed, timing, and precision; and dodging bullets thanks to well defined and clever tactics and strategies. Large companies who thought themselves safe after having cornered a market, soon find themselves bypassed by a smaller more agile companies, then disrupted and forced into bankruptcy. Entrepreneurs don't announce their moves, they are less transparent, born of a culture of secrecy, they make no sound, then suddenly appear and steal market share very quickly. Beware the entrepreneur whose back is against the wall - he has nothing to lose, the stomach knows no fear when screaming for victory.

BEST TO BEND WHILE IT IS A TWIG

A popular word used in business courses on entrepreneurship is the word agile. But flexibility in business is nothing new. Just as a blade of grass can bend with the wind, so the entrepreneur bends to better respond to market forces. The feat of success comes from remaining nimble, and constantly disrupting the market. Creating something new isn't easy, especially something that brings value to people's lives. An oak may be big and strong, but it can easily topple in the wind; rigidity isn't the answer in the entrepreneur's chaotic world. Learning to bend is not a simple skill, it doesn't come naturally, everybody would prefer to be an oak. Yet, for a startup, this is precisely the wrong strategy. Remaining nimble in the early days of a startup is a competitive advantage, a time when it's important to constantly reinvent, pivot, and remain agile.

THEY HAVE NEED OF A BROOM THAT SWEEPS THE HOUSE WITH A TURF

Being deadly honest with themselves is a prerequisite for entrepreneurs; revealing personal flaws which might get in the way of making sound rational decisions. An entrepreneur needs to be able to count on themselves and their team. Knowing themselves, soul-searching, resolving issues, is one of the most important and not often talked about requirements for success. Self-doubt is deadly. Taking a broom to personal insecurities, fears, bad habits becomes necessary as the startup needs to be the center of attention. It's not possible to have a drinking problem; it's not possible to have anger issues; it's not possible to be dishonest. The list can be long of behavior traits and bad habits which entrepreneurs would do best to master and eliminate. Running a company can be a daunting voyage of self-discovery. It's a good habit to buy a broom, keep it inside the mind, and use it often.

THE BEST IS BEST CHEAP

Entering into an already crowded market is challenging for an entrepreneur. The market is fraught with threats and barriers to entry - progress should never be direct but oblique. Rival companies defend themselves against potential competitors, but guerrilla tactics attempt to smoke them out from behind their defenses, surround them, dig tunnels under the defenses - anything to destabilize and overcome. Strategies can include lowering prices to compete, but price wars are risky, when margins and cash are needed to survive - it's better to enter a crowded market with new technologies, and use innovation to threaten rivals' dominant positions. Taking customers from rivals by offering better value and focusing on new and better benefits - this helps build positive cash flow, which can be reinvestment into more innovation, the indirect strategy is less cheap.

BEST IS BEST CHEAP, IF YOU HIT NOT THE NAIL

Marketing can be similar to a shell game - to confuse the player as to where lies the value. Creating the illusion the pea is where it isn't, the mis-perception is so strong, the solution seemingly so obvious, that players are convinced they'll win the next time, and they keep playing. Marketers are good at seducing with certain products and services, creating the illusion of high perceived value, when in fact the product is cheap and will soon break - the customer has the illusion of certainty, having gotten a good deal, even when they never actually hit the nail on the head. Yet they continue to play the game because they feel they've won something, they feel happy. In this manipulation, there's a sleight of hand, a trick of the mind, getting customers to focus on the wrong hand - they get their trick, and the entrepreneur makes his profit. Between the two of them, the nail is indeed driven home

MAKE THE BEST OF A BAD BARGAIN

It is possible to rip victory from the jaws of defeat. In the heat of battle entrepreneurs make mistakes and negotiate bad deals, missing out on a bargain, making bad decisions. How they recover, get back on their feet, determines just how seriously their error affects them. Denying the mistake, blaming others, is a setup to make the mistake again, and again. Mistakes are always going to be a part of running a company, its how they learn from them, renegotiate, and reposition themselves, that determines their ability to survive and prosper. A bad bargain may have been struck with a stakeholder a first time, by understanding the error, they won't make the same mistake twice. Mistakes can even be considered a form of success, if learned from. It's never too late to recover from a bad bargain, but never possible to always blaming others.

BETTER UNTAUGHT
THAN ILL-TAUGHT

Becoming an entrepreneur requires unlearning a lot of bad habits, relearning lost skills, learning new skills thought useless, and learning about learning. Most importantly, it's critical to keep an open mind. Many academic studies attempt to classify personality types best adapted to being an entrepreneur. The research is based on observing practicing entrepreneurs, who've succeeded and failed. For instance, learning to think creatively, becoming socially competent, or self-confident, resourceful, manipulative, persuasive. Some skills are harder to learn than others, and formed habits are difficult to unlearn or change, but an open mind and thoughtfulness help, to test their assumptions and reflect on their decisions. It's never too late to change course, take a step back, and apply new thoughts and new strategies, in order to move two steps forward.

BEWARE OF HAD I WISHED

Entrepreneurs shouldn't ruminate over what they wished they could have, should have, would have done differently. What matters is what they do in the present and the plan for the future. Past mistakes can be recoverable with the right attitude. They make-do with resources at hand; the planets are never always perfectly aligned, there is no right time, right tool, right customer, right product. It's about capabilities available now, and acting to the best of their abilities, with an eye on consequences, but without being able to predict the future. Regret feeds defeatism and lowers confidence, past mistakes must be quickly forgotten and better outcomes secured with better decision-making and problem-solving. Being in the present contributes to freeing the mind of fear; a practical mind, common sense, skills and competence, help to come up with better ideas and more effective new strategies to eliminate all regret and wishful thinking.

DO AS YOUR BIDDEN, AND YOU'LL NEVER BEAR BLAME

Nobody ever said that customers are easy to deal with, especially when things don't go their way. If a promise is made, then the expectation is that it be kept. If you make a commitment, honor it. Falling short of this simple business rule is inviting the wrath of the customer and the reputation as unreliable and a flake. In an age of social media customer feedback is more public than ever, it's nearly impossible to hide from poor conduct: Suppliers who renege on their commitments: manufacturing lead time, quality assurance, delivery time put the entire supply chain at risk, this can mean life and death to a business. The clock works because the moving parts deliver on their promises. If everyone does their job, there's no blame game to play, the work gets done by motivated, reliable professionals; the product is delivered and the profits made. Just as customers don't do business with flakes, neither do entrepreneurs.

BIRCHEN TWIGS
BREAK NO RIBS

In isolation, a problem may have the strength of a twig and cause no real damage, but repeated and combined with other small problems, can have the force to break a rib. It's important to nip problems in the bud before they grow out of control. Efficiently managing a company isn't only about what's quantifiable and measurable, but seemingly smaller, more subtle issues, such as managing time, risk and change. Poor organization, poor prioritizing, let alone denying reality, laziness and procrastination directly contribute to poor management. Staying on top of problems as they occur means more time can be spent dealing with solutions and profits. Twigs may be harmless and easily dealt with, however small buds tend to grow on twigs; caring for the twig is about keeping a watchful eye on its buds: eliminating budding problems before they can pack a punch, and nurturing those which will flourish into beautiful flowers and profitable fruits.

BIRDS OF A FEATHER
FLOCK TOGETHER

On the one hand, if the birds are customers, the entrepreneur benefits from having them flock together, according to their tastes, habits, personalities - marketing will then be about positioning, product differentiation, segmentation, targeting the flocks to maximize profit. On the other hand, if the birds are other entrepreneurs flocking towards the same business idea, it's a warning sign threatening the bottom line, and a signal to start adjusting the strategy. The entrepreneurs job is to scan the market in search of flocks, or provoking the grouping of new flocks, and to identify which are threats and which are opportunities. Serial entrepreneurs are good bird watchers, they love the hunt, and able to determine future possibilities and performance based on their wing span, beak size, coloration and migration patterns.

A BIRD IN THE HAND IS BETTER THAN TWO IN THE BUSH

Success as an entrepreneur doesn't come from one big gain, one massive victory; rather it's the result of many small actions, seemingly insignificant, easily missed, unappreciated. It's tempting to think that more or bigger is better, offers more value, or deserves all our attention. Only a small bird might be enough just to get started, when a big fat one is unavailable. Entrepreneurs make do with what they have, just to move the ball forward. Not all birds are equal opportunities, some will be duds, including the big one's; at least with the small birds the successes might be small , but then so are the failures. Small failures are more manageable than risking it all on one big action which could be one big failure. A step, in the right direction, is a start, even if at first a small step, which combined with other small steps make a big step. What's important is stability and sustainable growth over time.

'TIS AN ILL BIRD THAT BETRAYS ITS OWN NEST

The bird destroys its nest in order to improve on it - this is creative destruction; not to do so would be a betrayal; by doing so he's loyal to his reputation as an entrepreneur. Most birds keep adding layers to existing nests, rather than destroy to re-create. With creative destruction, each iteration of the nest offers improvements, a stronger foundation, a more efficient building technique, new features added to make life easier and more comfortable for raising children. All this takes more effort, but offers more satisfaction. With the increased experience the bird can build a new nest in less time than all other birds. Soon enough, the other birds approach the "ill" bird and hire him to build them a new nest in no time at all. As an entrepreneur, the "ill" bird now can launch an architecture firm, and make all his hard work pay off; until another "ill" bird comes along, and starts destroying the old in a new way, all over again.

EVERY BIRD MUST HATCH HER OWN EGG

Resisting the urge to start as soon as possible is an important discipline for a nascent entrepreneur. It's better to take the time to prepare well and keep the day job at first; the better the preparation the less the perspiration later on. When preparing the business plan, the brainstorming and planning stages are the most important, can take time, and goes through many iterations. The mission and vision amounts to wishful thinking if a strong plan isn't prepared carefully. There may be pressure from friends and family, questioning whether there ever will be a launch, but no move should be made until the entrepreneur's good and ready. Emotions should never get in the way; it's always wiser to wait for reason and facts to give the green light; resisting temptations to jump the gun is hard but necessary. Only he will know when it's time to launch, based on his research, the business plan, focus group feedback, his financials and his state of mind.

THE BIRD THAT CAN SING, AND WILL NOT SING, MUST BE MADE TO SING

Launching a new company doesn't have to cost much, bootstrapping is not just about not requiring large bank rolls to fund the launch, its about learning how to organize and prioritize. A bird can be made to sing if the right conditions exist for it to sing. If any critical element is missing the bird will not sing. Better to find out early on what are those missing elements might be. Stress may cause the bird to no to sing, so it's best to calm down and learn to be more confident. Running a business is stressful, not only because of the time it takes to research and develop, not because of the financial stakes, the long hours, the dedication, commitment and passion - but also because psychology, self-motivation, self-esteem are complex impulses which can't be controlled as easily as flipping a switch. Preparing the mind is part of that process, this cannot be forced; the bird will sing when it's ready, and when it is it, will sing beautifully.

SMALL BIRDS MUST
HAVE MEAT

It's all relative, to a small startup, the market appears much larger than to a bigger more established company. What the startup needs is an idea that solves a problem and helps the company grow; ideas are like meat. With the right idea, a startup can reduce the perception of a massive market, and grow comfortable with the big picture. Large companies are burdened by their size, making them more structurally rigid, risk averse and slow to react. Small birds, fed correctly, energized with proper meat, can fly in and out, and through the legs of its bigger rivals. It comes down to energized ideas and designing products that seduce stakeholders and capture as much market share as possible. As the startup grows, it hires on more small birds, to keep the company lean; and is scours the market in search of new opportunities, new ideas, new sources of energy.

BIRTH IS MUCH, BUT BREEDING MORE

Drive, is what gets entrepreneurs to push themselves, sometimes to the breaking point. There's nothing wrong with taking a step back, or sideways, to consolidate gains before the next push forward. These threshold pauses provide time to reflect, regroup, align with objectives, focus on weaknesses, strengths, digest gains - before launching onto the next leg forward. It's quality growth they're after. Entrepreneurs improve because with experience, their ideas are of higher breeding, they are more methodical, careful with how they grow. The company starts to become more aware of its brand image, it's gone beyond the stage of worrying about it's survival, and starts thinking of its legacy, or breeding an image for itself. A field of flowers is made up of individual flowers, each blossoming and fighting for survival - but together, in the field, they're a vision of great beauty, as all the flowers work together in perfect harmony.

IF YOU CANNOT BITE, NEVER SHOW YOUR TEETH

There's nothing like a confident communications message to inspire customers to want to buy into a new product or service. Startups that are passive are never able to reach their goals; startups that are proactive, twist and swerve as they struggle forward to make good on their promises to customers, are the one's that prosper. There are many bad ideas that become successful because the entrepreneur and her team showed the confidence required to convince and inspire customers. On the other hand, many great ideas tanked, leading the startup straight into bankruptcy, because rather than pro-actively sell the product, the entrepreneur assumed customers would automatically recognize the brilliant innovation and throw money at it. Customers want to buy a story, not just the product. A story must be active, engaging, exciting, demonstrate authenticity, show real people struggling to succeed and change the world. Customers will buy a hero's journey - a product with spirit and soul, a story with bite.

HE THAT BITES ON EVERY WEED, MUST HAVE KNOWLEDGE OF POISON

Settling on an idea and going with it, isn't as easy as it seems - it's the outcome of a process of choices, selections and decisions. For the nascent entrepreneur the temptation is to look at a problem from a very general perspective - this makes the choices vast and the selection process confusing. General assumptions must be whittled down to specifics. Ideas start out very broad, very general, but a product on the shelf provides a solution to one problem. At first, it's important not to try to please all the customers everywhere, just some of them in specific areas; it's OK to start small, and scale later. Starting overly general is expensive; becoming an expert or hiring them to cover every sector is ruinous; a strategy that spreads scarce resources too thinly, death by poisoning. The first most specific skill an entrepreneur should learn is how to think in specifics, focusing on specific details, and matching them to specific needs and problems in the market.

BLACK WILL TAKE
NO OTHER HUE

Success as an entrepreneur is helped by learning to develop the right attitude, this implies the ability to change. Not everyone is comfortable with change, it can hurt; yet, it's difficult to clear the mind and focus on the present time when carrying around baggage from the past. The mind must be clear and focused on running the company, and immune to annoying negative thoughts from personal relationships gone wrong, old friends who drag everything into the gutter, jealous family members. It's important to separate the personal from the professional, especially as many entrepreneurs work from home. Going as far as cutting out friends and family who rather than helping and promoting, act selfishly and jealously to keep the nascent entrepreneur down. This can be difficult, after a lifetime of bad habits, but it's essential. Black energy absorbs everything around it - when an entrepreneur needs to focus on creating and organizing a world full of color.

A BLACK HEN LAYS
A WHITE EGG

Some of the best opportunities lie below the surface, and require from the entrepreneur the curiosity and determination to scratch beneath it. Success depends on originality, entrepreneurs scratch beneath the surface of opportunities in search of the unique, to offer customers value beyond the surface. It takes extra effort to dig deeper, organization, perspiration and determination. A business concept that remains all on the surface ends up offering a bland, boring, repetitive, uninspiring service with which customers can't identity. A weak product and service offers rivals an opportunity to enter the market with a closer approximation of customer needs. Customers want personalization, they want to feel something special when shopping, they want to know that even if on the outside the hen is black, what they get on the inside will surprise them, enhance their shopping experience and make them happy.

THEY HAVE NEED OF A BLESSING WHO KNEEL TO A THISTLE

If starting and running a company were easy everyone would succeed; yet, according to statistics, most companies go bankrupt within the first few years of existence. Success is hard, and prickly, like a thistle. Too succeed, requires hugging the thistle, enduring the pain; in the end it's a small price to pay, beating the odds and becoming successful. Despite the bite of the thistle, the entrepreneur never shows the pain to the customer, he remains professional, showing only enthusiasm and optimism, even in the face of adversity. These are tests, which the entrepreneur must overcome; and if ever he lets down his guard, the thistle will be sure to poke him until he cries. Entrepreneurs learn to grow comfortable with the thistles, which never leave them alone, always at the ready for a prick. Comfort and friendship with the thistle is what defines entrepreneur's who succeed, from those who quit. Success is not given, it's earned.

BLOW FIRST, AND
SIP AFTERWARDS

In the excitement of wanting to impress friends
and family, desperate to demonstrate self-worth
and self-efficacy, entrepreneurs are carried forward
relentlessly by their emotions: impatience, ambition
and arrogance. Unless they're lucky, and that's
never been a reliable strategy, they either burnout
or burn-down. It's better to let reason and strategy
do the thinking, rather than let emotions lead,
when carefully planning the release of a product
by testing the market. Ideas are hypotheses which,
until proven robust, remain abstract fantasies based
on wishful thinking and delusional speculations.
Rushing to market on the basis of a mere speculation
is a sure way of increasing risks. Entrepreneurs are
in the risk reduction game. Such actions may feed
the ego, but the feeling of euphoria is short lived.
Lead with strategy and calculation, progress slowly
and cautiously, and let hot ideas cool down, lest they
end up burning a hole in the wallet.

A BLOT IS NO BLOT
UNLESS IT BE HIT

A great way to move up the learning curve when launching a new idea is to learn from mistakes made by others. Case studies are a great resource, providing great insight into what other companies did right or wrong. Knowledge provides the power to change course, make better decisions, plan more effectively. Access to information and knowledge helps mitigate risks, understand the mistakes of others, offers important clues, and helps entrepreneurs adapt their tactics and strategies to sidestep potential blots; the more blots made by others, the better. It's all about eliminating the probability of future errors. Success includes navigating through the blots, using a map created by studying blots made by others. Such road-maps, when used, and carefully implemented, act as a lifesaver as the entrepreneur crosses the minefields of the competitive market; allowing entrepreneurs to succeed where others failed.

BLUSHING IS
VIRTUE'S COLOR

Providing excellent customer service is never a waste of time. Success is made easier by being a people person, not shying away but embracing customers with compassion and caring. Offering good service comes form the heart, it's about creating a bond with customers, building relationships and repeat business. This takes lots of effort over time, applied repeatedly, to build trust, and positive word-of-mouth. Entrepreneurs make such behavior part of the company's core values, to distinguish themselves from competitors who don't, and feel good about themselves. In return customers are happier becoming advocates publicizing and promoting its products and services - it's a way of saying thanks. Superficial uncaring customer service is a colorless form of virtue, cheap and self-serving; whereas caring invites compliments and rewards - success comes from a lot of blushing.

GREAT BOAST
SMALL ROAST

Marketing is a subtle game, and tends to work in paradoxical ways. The entrepreneur who shouts at the top of his lungs that he's the best, the cheapest, the most qualified, the best at everything, but then under-delivers, provides a shoddy service and rips off customers, is on a sure road to failure. Marketing is a subtle game of push and pull with customers. Being too pushy might work in the short run, but building a serious business for the long run requires building a customer based on trust and credibility. A pushy pitch might work on some and in certain circumstances, but doesn't inspire trust. Marketing is about people, psychology; soft selling is always more effective, and entrepreneurs must learn its rules. There are more effective ways of selling confidence, without aggression and hard power. Entrepreneurs have a choice, but at the end of the day, the size of the roast on the table, will tell the whole story.

THE NEARER THE BONE THE SWEETER THE FLESH

Building trust is one of the most important tasks at which entrepreneurs must excel. The greater the honesty the closer the entrepreneur gets to the sweet flesh off the bone of the consumer market. Customers are wary of buying a product from an entrepreneur whose intention is to give them the nasty bits off the bone. There's no worse feeling than being ripped off; to avoid this, customers will shop around, read feedback from other customers before making the plunge. Up to the entrepreneur to communicate what part of the meat he's selling. Customers are forgiving if they understand what they're getting. Many customers won't want to pay a premium price for the sweet meant, but at least they have a choice. Success as a startup is understanding where on the marketing landscape the entrepreneur chooses to position himself. Customers looking for value are often happy enough to be near the bone.

HE THAT GOES A BORROWING GOES A SORROWING

Learning money management skills is important for entrepreneurs. On the back of hopes and dreams of future profits, entrepreneurs often fall into the trap of borrowing and then thinking that money borrowed is the same as money made. All money is created the same, but there's a difference between positive and negative equity. Building a startup strategy around debt is risky, especially if the idea doesn't work out. One of the principles of bootstrapping it to make do with little startup debt; instead using creativity, wit and brawn to launch products that generate profits as soon as possible; to break-even almost immediately, and re-invest the profits into product development and marketing. Ideally, a product or service value proposition should be able to stand on its own two feet, without needing the crutch of other people's money; a great idea should sell itself. Debt is useful only once an idea has proven itself, to scale.

THEY THAT ARE BOUND MUST OBEY

Entrepreneurs are contrarian by nature, disruptors, iconoclasts, challenging established rules, bending, breaking, being laughed at, until they're proven right. What they seek is independence from the routine, from being someone else's employee, following their rules, abiding by their policies, helping themselves become rich. Becoming an entrepreneur is like breaking out of jail, escaping from the oppression of being a wage slave and living from paycheck to paycheck. They're willing to take the risk, even if many "escapees" eventually get caught, and are thrown back in the wage slave jail. Once out, and to stay out, the entrepreneur must carefully plan, calculate, making choices that are strategic and tactical, cover his steps and never get "caught". Remaining independent means resisting bad habits, building self-confidence and work ethic discipline to remain "free". Independence isn't the natural order of things, it's the contrarian exception.

LET EVERY MAN PRAISE THE BRIDGE HE GOES OVER

There are many types of bridges entrepreneur's use to get from an idea to a market. It isn't necessary each time to reinvent the wheel; there are plenty of existing bridges a bootstrapping entrepreneur can cross: non-profit organizations existing to pride free advice, communities of retired entrepreneurs acting as mentors, government agencies, online courses, books. Some bridges are best used for building a franchise, a turnkey operation helping to get to profitability more quickly, lowering the risks of failure; others lead to the land of venture capital, or main street shops, vendor vans, and hundreds of other entrepreneurial possibilities. Not all bridges are created equal, some less traveled by lead to fabulous opportunities. Some bring lifestyle, others are passions bringing few rewards but lots of joy; or rickety rope bridges with cracked slates, collapsing half-way to the other side. Choose the bridge wisely, and sing its praise once successful.

BRIDGES WERE MADE FOR WISE MEN TO WALK OVER, AND FOR FOOLS TO RIDE OVER

Success comes from being in the here and now, and not off somewhere else, unable to concentrate on the task at hand. Entrepreneurship is a slow walk across the bridge, to notice the cracks, fissures, problems, opportunities. The entrepreneur may rush across, with eyes cast on distant dreams, but then miss the early symptoms of future problems. Small fissures have a nasty tendency of getting worse over time. Speed is a false friend, many entrepreneurs thinking that getting to their destinations quickly will somehow help them win, when slow and steady notices the fissures, builds deeper knowledge, stronger relationships, and sustainability. When taking the time, better opportunities are identified, more time is spent on details; for rush jobs it's better to outsource to fools who rush around like headless chickens.

A BRIBE WILL ENTER WITHOUT KNOCKING

The term bribe is a relative one. While in some cultures bribes are a form of corruption and frowned upon, in others, there's no other way to conduct business. In high risk environments, where contract law is shaky and corruption abounds, bribing is the price for opening doors, gaining favor, winning the contract, building trust; in this context, not to accept a bribe is considered suspicious even stupid. Different cultures and their traditions, interpret ethical dimensions in different ways, in their bid to gain an advantage: in an environment where everyone accepts bribes, not accepting a bribe becomes a relative competitive disadvantage. In those cultures, bribes are just another business strategy, where laws were weak and poorly enforced - it doesn't need an introduction, it takes front and center stage in any negotiation, it's always a welcome guest and never needs to knock.

BRING NOT A BAGPIPE TO
A MAN IN TROUBLE

Being in tune with how to manage his niche, the entrepreneur becomes the indispensable element in running a specialized company. He's worked hard to find the tune that works, getting the customers to buy. Years of tweaking, learning to play a difficult instrument, earned him his just rewards. Others have tried and failed, he alone persisted. In running a company, there are many skills that take a long time to master, to become an expert in the field: marketing skills, money management, inventory, design, people skills. Being an entrepreneur involves being a continuous student, always learning new skills, practicing, perfecting. A man in trouble who's not prepared for when a crisis hits, is vulnerable, and depends on expensive outside help to fix the problem. Self-reliance is important to entrepreneurs, they'll make the effort and learn to play the bagpipe if it gives them an advantage in the market.

A BROKEN SACK WILL HOLD NO CORN

It's far easier to lose money than to make it. Businesses are money hemorrhaging machines, and entrepreneurs try to make a profit, they plug the holes in the sack, and stop the hemorrhage from getting out of control. Together, various forms of costs, whether variable or fixed, conspire to suck money from the entrepreneurs wallet at a speed greater than her ability to fill it. She understands that to make money, the she has to spend it, but expects a return greater than the expense, knowing that a startup is a sack of corn full of holes. Not failing is stemming the outgoing flow of money, and increasing the inflow, consistently and sustainably. It's a lot of work and keeps the entrepreneur busy, she needs help just managing that process, which costs more money, he has to hire accountants, and managers, to make the sack thicker, plugging holes at a faster rate; hiring sales people helps make more money, fix the levees, and manage the locks. It's all about flow.

FULL OF COURTESY, FULL OF CRAFT

It isn't a naive and innocent entrepreneur who succeeds, it isn't a tricky and disingenuous on who fails easily. Being friendly is pleasant and important, being crafty and savvy can be the secret sauce that helps keep the company afloat. All depends on the type of business, but with negotiation being at the heart of all business, knowing the rules of the game is important. Soft power is far more effective that hard power, a smile will get an entrepreneur farther than a scold, politeness is a code of good conduct and civilized behavior - but these do signal weakness, but high context craft. Different cultures have different approaches to doing business, some are indirect others not, some hard others have softer edges, some are angled and sharp while other have more rounded corners. Being away of context helps avoid misunderstandings and provides the visibility to understand the other parties intentions, and how best to absorb the style of negotiation, pivot, deflect, and re-position for a win/win.

WHAT IS A POUND OF BUTTER AMONG A KENNEL OF HOUNDS

A guaranteed way of going bankrupt is to make a product that is ill-adapted to the target market, a product nobody wants or understands. Surprisingly, this happens all the time, as entrepreneurs underestimate the needs and desires of customers, and don't do their research. An entrepreneur's subjective opinion is as dangerous as having the wrong product for the wrong market, being objective helps keep analysis real, to positively align the relevant factors which help the business succeed. It's the customer's needs and wants that matter in the end. Focusing on the customer means the entrepreneur will connect the dots correctly and discover innovative new ways of making bones out of butter, hardened and retaining their creamy white surface texture - a product the dogs would recognize. It isn't the entrepreneur who'll be eating the bones, he'll be reaping the profits, to each his own bone.

THAT WHICH WILL NOT BE BUTTER, MUST BE MADE INTO CHEESE

Stubbornness is a double-edged sword - just as it may help it can also hinder. Future success is impossible to guarantee, but can be predicted based on present behavior, assumptions and actions. When it looks like commercial activity is turning south, when the cash flow dashboard starts sending out warning signs, it's time to change course. Sticking to a plan that doesn't work is the wrong kind of stubbornness. Managing change, is part of what helps entrepreneurs succeed. They are change making agents, born of change and symbols of change to unsuspecting rivals, customers and other stakeholders. The company survives because it constantly reinvents itself and promises something better, newer, cheaper, higher quality, better adapted. Change is the message, the entrepreneur the white knight, the promise of the new idea, the new value; turning butter to cheese and cheese to milk, that's the kind of stubbornness he should have.

WHO BUYS, HAS NEED OF A HUNDRED EYES; WHO SELLS, HAS ENOUGH OF ONE

Buyers are increasingly discerning, especially given the power they have to search the internet, and review products before buying. Offline pricing information is usually very vague and opaque, unless the seller shares that information, which they usually don't. Thanks to the internet however, customers can easily compare and cross-reference prices and reviews, and arrive at a pretty good idea of fair value. When launching their online companies, entrepreneurs offer customers subscription services with the lowest possible price - free. The freemium model says, the basic service is free, but if you want some bells and whistles you'll have to upgrade to a paying service. Immediately customers see where they stand, there are no hidden costs; it's an open and transparent system that screams trust and respect. With the arrival of the internet, customers now have ten thousand eyes.

BUYING AND SELLING IS BUT WINNING AND LOSING

Everyone is someone's seller and buyer. There are many ways for entrepreneurs to make money. Making a product and selling it with a handsome margin is one way; or bundling a service along with the product is how to make extra; offering discounts and guaranteeing great value, builds brand loyalty which leads to repeat business. It's important to know how to both sell and buy; getting it wrong will either alienate the customer, or the supplier. Knowing how to buy and sell makes the difference between winning and losing. Poor negotiating when placing a purchase order puts the squeeze on the startup's profit margin, or commits the entrepreneur to an expensive lease on a commercial site. Everything doesn't have to be win/lose; good partnerships with all stakeholders are about the win/win - along the entire supply chain to the final customer - the losing part is eliminated entirely.

A POUND OF CARE
WILL NOT PAY
AN OUNCE OF DEBT

Promoting a startup when launching can be daunting, and expensive. Adopting the wrong marketing strategy can be a disaster as the entrepreneur has limited resources and may not get a second chance. Advertisers are care delivery services, but their fees represent a heavy price per ounce of care. Guerrilla marketing tries to get the care message directly to the customer, lowering the need for, and even bypassing, the high-priced middle man of advertising. It's possible with a powerful marketing narrative. Customers don't care what it costs to get them to notice the product, they just want to see the product and hear the story. If they care, they'll buy the product. The story of a struggling entrepreneur overcoming all obstacles and challenges is a powerful narrative appealing to people's sense of empathy and care. If the product is high quality, and the story is good, then the product will sell itself. Caring is still free.

CARE WILL KILL A CAT

As an entrepreneur it's important to be organized, methodical, attentive to detail, think and move fast. Many aspects of running a business take time: build relationships, inspiring trust, attention to detail, being focused - they may take time and resources, but they're the kind of caring without which the entrepreneur can't survive. So learning to manage time becomes important, depending on the strategy, time can be compressed. With enough repetition and experience entrepreneur's become more efficient and are able to combine speed with care, detail with efficiency - they become more productive, providing more care in less time. They have shifted the value of time, where taking time becomes a strength, appealing to a customer who wants more time to make a decision, who needs more caring. Leveraging time compresses time, and allows more time to care, and pay special attention to details that help the business flourish.

A MUFFLED CAT IS NO GOOD MOUSER

There can be no doubt that success is greatly enhanced by craftiness, common sense and good planning. Success is helped by not holding back and instead throwing the kitchen sink at the tasks at hand, to reach the full potential of the entrepreneurial experience and give the startup a fighting chance to succeed. To catch a mouse, a cat becomes an expert, he starts with a plan, which he adapts according to unforeseen opportunities and threats. He gives it his all because he has everything to lose - he has to feed himself and his family. So take off the muzzle, be bold, think out of the box, connect dots others wouldn't dare, it's what makes a good mouser. Work hard to develop the skills, don't do things half-way, but 150%, seizing the moment! The mouse is adept at evading, so what, become adept at catching, and be loud about it! If the cat is shy, or the mouse too crafty, then the cat gets nothing and starves. Failure isn't an option.

WHEN THE CAT IS AWAY, THE MICE WILL PLAY

If the entrepreneur doesn't control the company's image and reputation, then others will. The marketplace is an aggressive place and rivals can be brutal. Success can make others jealous, so they start to play dirty, spreading rumors that damage the companies image, undermining reputation. Even if an entrepreneur intends to play fair, to not defend his company's reputation is allowing others to control the narrative. If attacked, take off the gloves, and use the attack as an opportunity to enhance your image as a trusting partner and socially responsible actor. Not defending oneself against the spread of false rumors, letting the mice run amok, can be construed by loyal core customers as not caring enough to reassure them; they become confused and lose faith. The cat must turn the situation around, making the attacks backfire, hurting the mice more than him. The threat of a counter-attack alone can be dissuasive, suing them for slander will also work.

I'LL KEEP NO MORE CATS THAN WILL CATCH MICE

Finding the right talent is one of the most difficult tasks for entrepreneurs. It's important to find the right balance between having too many employees whose talents overlap and end up getting in each others way, and hiring too few, whose skills may complement each other but are stretched so thin they end up demotivated and burned out. Hiring new talent is expensive, resource management is no joke and must be proactively managed. The type of industry will determine the best policy to adopt when hiring new talent. Creative industries thrive off of many cooks in the kitchen, bumping into each other, connecting dots, working in teams, generating new ideas to which they can attach their names, and enhance both their own reputation and that of the company. Retaining talent, once trained, is crucially important, not doing so can put the startup's future at risk.

HE THAT LEAVES CERTAINTY AND STICKS TO CHANCE

Dealing with ambiguity is an important requirement for entrepreneurs. Luck is risk with a positive outcome; the reverse is bad luck - placing the future of the company in the hands of luck is not a plan, it's a gamble. Risk management cannot be left to luck or bad luck, it must be made more secure, more certain. Careful planning increases the certainty of risky situations, failing to plan is planning to fail. An entrepreneur is comfortable with ambiguity as long as it's under control, uncertainties are more certain when an effective strategy provides greater visibility. If chance happens to come along that's a bonus. A good plan should eliminate luck entirely, and keep at bay the potential for bad luck. Any ambiguity should be controlled and calculated, so that it contributes to furthering the plan; the best luck is the one the entrepreneur creates with the help of a robust plan.

CHANGE OF PASTURE MAKES FAT COWS

Perhaps one of the most exciting times for entrepreneurs is when they're starting out. It's also the most daunting, stressful and difficult period. At this stage the calves are thin, feeling not very confident. His objective is to get to greener pastures, and he doesn't intend to allow anything to get in his way. It's important to have an objective, clearly indicated by the vision and mission set out in the business plan. Desire helps pull the entrepreneur forward towards success; helping him overcome obstacles, picking himself back up, until the cows are fat. His passion and drive are fueled by creative and strategic thinking, he's determined to get his calves to greener pastures, to fatten them up, and produce the best possible milk, cheese and meat in the land. He dreams of fat cows, he dreams of success, he's an entrepreneur, he's in the business of fattening cows.

CHARITY BEGINS AT HOME

Long gone are the days when entrepreneurs could afford to be rude to their customers, caring not for their interests, and instead expecting the customers to be thankful for the opportunity to shop in their establishment. Today, if customers detect any attitude they walk, they'll surf over to a different shop on the internet, at the click of their mouse. The world belongs to customers, they shop not because they feel charitable, but because they feel happy, and like the shopping experience in a particular place. Entrepreneurs whose mindsets aren't attuned to these realities are setting themselves up for the harsher realities of bankruptcy. Empathy, extroversion, agreeableness and conscientiousness are important mindsets for building relationships with customers - they help project a positive image, and create bonds of trust. Customers increasingly shop from home, and when an outside guest is welcomed, it's expected they behave respectfully.

WHEN GOOD CHEER IS LACKING, OUR FRIENDS WILL BE PACKING

Attitude is important when deciding to embark on the entrepreneurship adventure. Managing a company is hard enough without the added burden of negative thinking and general lack of good cheer. Success is aided by being a good people person, acting with respect and consideration. There is an inverse relationship between having a bad attitude and being successful. Dealing with anger, selfishness, or other forms of personality problems can send important stakeholders packing, they don't have to indulge such behavior. Entrepreneurs represent the face of the company, their performance and attitude matter when building an image of strength, stability and reliability. Positive thinking requires work and dedication, an openness to learn to listen carefully, accept criticism, and make changes before the negative energy takes over. Customers don't buy bad attitude, they buy positive solutions to problems; same with employees.

CHILDREN AND FOOLS
SPEAK THE TRUTH

One of the most important skills an entrepreneur can learn from a very early stage is learning to listen. Whether it be listening to customers, employees, mentors, or even themselves, feedback potentially provides important information vital to the company's prosperity. The skill to listen to feedback is particularly important, especially as it may go against existing assumptions and perceptions; there's no room for egotism. Because entrepreneurs are rushing around, knee-deep in their business, and everything seems to be working, it's tempting to discard external observations as irrelevant, when what might be irrelevant is their way of doing business. Success comes from reading future trends and shifting the company's strategy to capture and ride the wave of new needs and wants. Customers are an important source of information and knowledge about future trends, they provide lots of clues - but only captured when the entrepreneur stops talking and starts listening.

THE GREATEST CLERKS
ARE NOT ALWAYS
THE WISEST MEN

Sitting in contemplation, studying and reading about entrepreneurship isn't the same thing as its practice. Companies don't fail any less now that every self-respecting university offers a course in entrepreneurship. In a classroom, the stakes are never as high as in real life, there are no risks to calculate accurately since they're not real, no real obstacles and setbacks to test the character, and sharpen the wit. Some of the greatest entrepreneurs of all time never went to school, never read a 500 page book on entrepreneurship, their essays were the mistakes they made, their diploma their company's. Reality was their school, and they learned quickly how to maneuver, learning from mistakes and listening to advice given by mentors. Entrepreneurs aren't born, and they aren't made in school, they're forged in the trenches, and sculpted through action and reaction, they don't talk the talk, they walk the walk - they're not clerks, they're entrepreneurs.

HASTY CLIMBERS
HAVE SUDDEN FALLS

Doing a rush job makes no sense if the outcome is failure. Entrepreneurs aren't given road maps or clear objectives, nor the means and resources to get the job done. Often, they figure it out as they go, proceeding cautiously, methodically, with the help of a carefully outlined business plan, which takes time to write, goes through many iterations, and never reaches perfection. Entrepreneurs are always rushing, juggling everything at once, running out of time, and when they fall, when they encounter a setback, they panic because they have no time to spare, so they plow ahead hoping the problem will go away, but it grows and it starts to affect other areas of the company, then it becomes too late to fix the problem, which has reached crisis proportions, and finally ends up sinking the company. A business plan helps avoid mistakes that take time to fix, with more time and less rushed, entrepreneurs fall less, and have even more time to focus on success.

THE CLOCK GOES AS IT PLEASES THE CLERK

If the entrepreneur can't overcome her indecisiveness, if she can't discipline herself to properly manage her money, if she takes for granted the amazing freedom which being an entrepreneur represents, then she's setting herself up to having all of that managed by somebody else. To become the master of her destiny, set the pace, trend and time, she needs to prove she can handle herself as an entrepreneur. It's her actions that allow her to maintain control over her affairs and destiny. Her success comes from her ability to pivot when sensing she's on the wrong path, prepared for the unexpected; able to confront ambiguity because strategically positioned, capable of concise decisions-making, and acting out her plans. By calculating her moves carefully and taking decisive actions, she helps her ship afloat, and avoids losing control of her freedom and independence, remaining the master of her own clock.

A CLOSED MOUTH CATCHES NO FLIES

Testing ideas before a launch is an important step - a hypothesis for an idea needs feedback from potential customers, to gauge their interest, and forecast possible performance. The entrepreneur must craft a marketing and sales pitch which communicates the core purpose of a product or service, addressing specifically the exact benefits provided to the customer, the problem to be solved. Stakeholders want to hear the message directly from the owners, to feel their passion, understand their assumptions, and get involved early on. If it's a sweet idea, then like flies, stakeholders will come to feast. Many startups are able to raise capital from venture capitalists even when they haven't made a profit, simply on the strength of their pitch, their business model. Entrepreneurs are the faces of their startup, their mouth is the company's mouth. In order to catch all those flies, and feast on the buzz, it's best to walk around with an open mouth.

GLOWING COALS
SPARKLE OFTEN

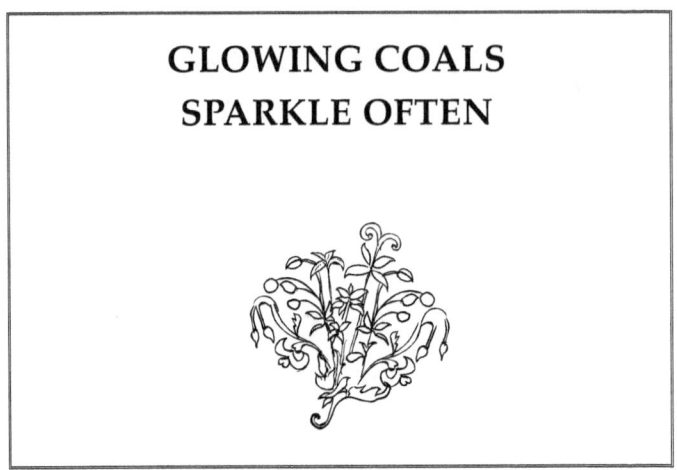

Before there can be any talk of starting a company there must be a reason, a purpose. Starting for the sake of starting doesn't feed the entrepreneur, perhaps only his ego. The decision to start a company is serious, the costs are high, as everyday spent running the startup could be spent elsewhere earning a paycheck. Preparation, by brainstorming ideas and finding what works and doesn't, is one of the most creative and strategic parts of being an entrepreneur. Glowing opportunities must be identified and then placed in the market to find the right fit. In the initial stages of brainstorming, ideas are wacky and freakish looking - research and tests help transform the idea into a workable business model, to create value and build a sustainable business. Some ideas will glow less than others, testing will reveal the winners from the losers, it's the only way to figure out whether an idea is merely piece of black coal, or has the potential of turning into a diamond.

YOU MUST CUT YOUR COAT ACCORDING TO YOUR CLOTH

Entrepreneurs are constrained by how much cloth they have to work with, resources are scarce, especially when they're starting out. Sometimes ideas are so ambitious, that turning them into reality is just impossible. The key is not to complicate but to simplify; finding ways of taking the idea and stripping it down to its bare essentials, and working on one aspect of the idea first, before moving onto others. Dreams can be very expensive and resource hungry, therefore, at first, it's better to focus on ideas that require fewer resources, and build capability little by little. Business plans help establish feasibility, and business models help test the idea in the marketplace, bouncing it off of customers and investors. Reality will cut the dream to size, and feedback will make sure it's relevant to actual needs, and practical enough to provide value and build wealth.

LET HIM THAT IS COLD BLOW THE COAL

Necessity is the mother of invention. Resourcefulness has a way of making an appearance in times of need, whether tinkering a repair, fixing a problem, improving performance, helping others. Entrepreneurs are constantly thinking of ways to improve processes, and create wealth doing so. If the problem is warmth, he'll come up with a solution, he'll burn the midnight oil doing it, driven by a sense of accomplishment, personal satisfaction and profit. In the end, it isn't the inspiration that makes the money, it's the perspiration. It's easy to underestimate the long grueling hours, the ups and downs, the strain on family and friends, the financial woes. But the need for warmth turns the perspiration into a quest to get to the other side of the barren mountain, and into the lush, fertile valley of warmth, happiness and prosperity. That's the dream that fuels the perspiration, and pushes the entrepreneur to constantly blow on that coal.

IN THE COLDEST FLINT
THERE IS HOT FIRE

Entrepreneurs take into their hands their own fates. Everyday will not be easy, but their resilience and determination will help them achieve their goals and turn their dreams into reality. The ability to think out-of-the-box is one of the most powerful tools available to the entrepreneur, constantly challenged and threatened with failure. This mental process is about reframing problems, and looking at them from different perspectives until a solution is found. Unpacking a problem and analyzing the different components helps identify what piece does what, understanding which one's to eliminate, which to invent. Once the pieces identified and made to better work together, commercial value is added by building a container and package around it, creating a product or service which can be marketed. Fire can be derived from flint, it starts by looking at the problem from different perspectives.

A RAGGED COLT MAY MAKE A GOOD HORSE

Ten thousand entrepreneurs will make the same discovery, only one will manage to turn it into a viable business. The process of taking an idea and transforming it into a value creating opportunity remains complex and available only when the right entrepreneur with the right skills and insight meets-up with the right idea, and looks at the problem in the right way. Entrepreneurs specialize in specific types of problems and spend their time trying to figure out configurations for solving them. They connect dots, which they gather from around themselves, inventing dots as they go, adding missing skills on the run, until they're able to successfully turn their experiment into a commercial product. The imagination sees value where others don't, the entrepreneur then finds the correct dot configuration: turning a ragged colt into a good horse, tweaking the dots until the right arrangement is found, and greater value is created.

A CLEAR CONSCIENCE
IS A SURE CARD

Family businesses represent a large percentage of small medium enterprises, they are more conservative, take less risks, offer stability, and this reassures customers. A family business will think as a team, it isn't the interest of one single member that matters, but the welfare of the entire group, making decisions together, and keeping each other in check. A family business is built for the long-run, building products and offering services that prove sustainable over time. They won't mobilize the efforts of the entire family to be in the business of ripping people off. Communicating family values and lifestyle to stakeholders helps build trust in the company, contributing to long-term loyalty and authenticity. Part of building a strong brand is providing stakeholders with a story to enrich and inspire their own lives and families. Doing business with a clear conscience and strong values is all about positive energy and love, these are truly sure cards.

GOOD COUNCIL NEVER COMES TOO LATE

There is no shame in turning to others for professional help to save the company from going bankrupt, or for better negotiating a big contract. Seeking help is neither admitting ignorance, nor a sign of weakness, on the contrary. Many entrepreneurs like to think they can do it all themselves, their startup an extension of their ego, their independence and self-reliance part of their persona. A powerful emotion, pride, has sunken many a ship, and must be conquered in order to unlock the benefits of seeking outside council. In a fast changing market environment, new techniques and ideas are constantly threatening the strategic positions of companies; new skills become old fast, and new talent, new insight, new advice, is needed to keep the company competitive. Entrepreneurs can't do it all, and need to turn to others for advice, to help in making accurate decisions and take effective actions.

MUCH CORN LIES UNDER THE STRAW THAT IS NOT SEEN

How does an entrepreneur know whether his actions account for the full potential of any given idea. It helps to carefully analyze the reactions of customers and other stakeholders, and monitor financial statements. Depending on the product or service, entrepreneurs seek out the sweet spot: few customers providing most of the profit. Not so few that he becomes dependent on only one or two clients; but few enough that he can run his business and have some time left over for a private life. Finding the perfect match between product or service offered and the precise needs and expectations of customers is hitting the sweet spot, where a product reaches its full potential, until there's no corn left lying under the straw; every piece has been found and is accounted for. For every customer, there's a perfect product and visa versa. This is the holy grail where entrepreneurs and their company's can hit the cruise control and their company becomes sustainable over time.

A FRIEND IN COURT IS WORTH A PENNY IN A MAN'S PURSE

When searching for opportunities it's important to cast a wide net; networking and communicating are two large enough nets. An entrepreneur should always be meeting new people, networking and casting out new nets. On the one hand meeting the right people can lead to the brainstorming of a new idea, a new opportunity; on the other, people with ideas and projects will approach an entrepreneur whom they remember meeting at a conference, a party, through a friend, through the friend of a friend. It's the grapevine, and it works in a very powerful way, exponentially in fact: one person speaks to two, who each speak to two and so on, and pretty soon thousands of people are involved. The internet has magnified this process, and provided powerful networking and communication tools for schmoozing. Having the right friends in the right place helps move the ball forward more quickly, resolve bottlenecks, provide advice, capital, new ideas, positive energy, friendship.

Other titles by Alexander F. Goldsborough:

Aesop for Entrepreneurs

Aesop for Entrepreneurs, Fables 26-50

www.aesopforentrepreneurs

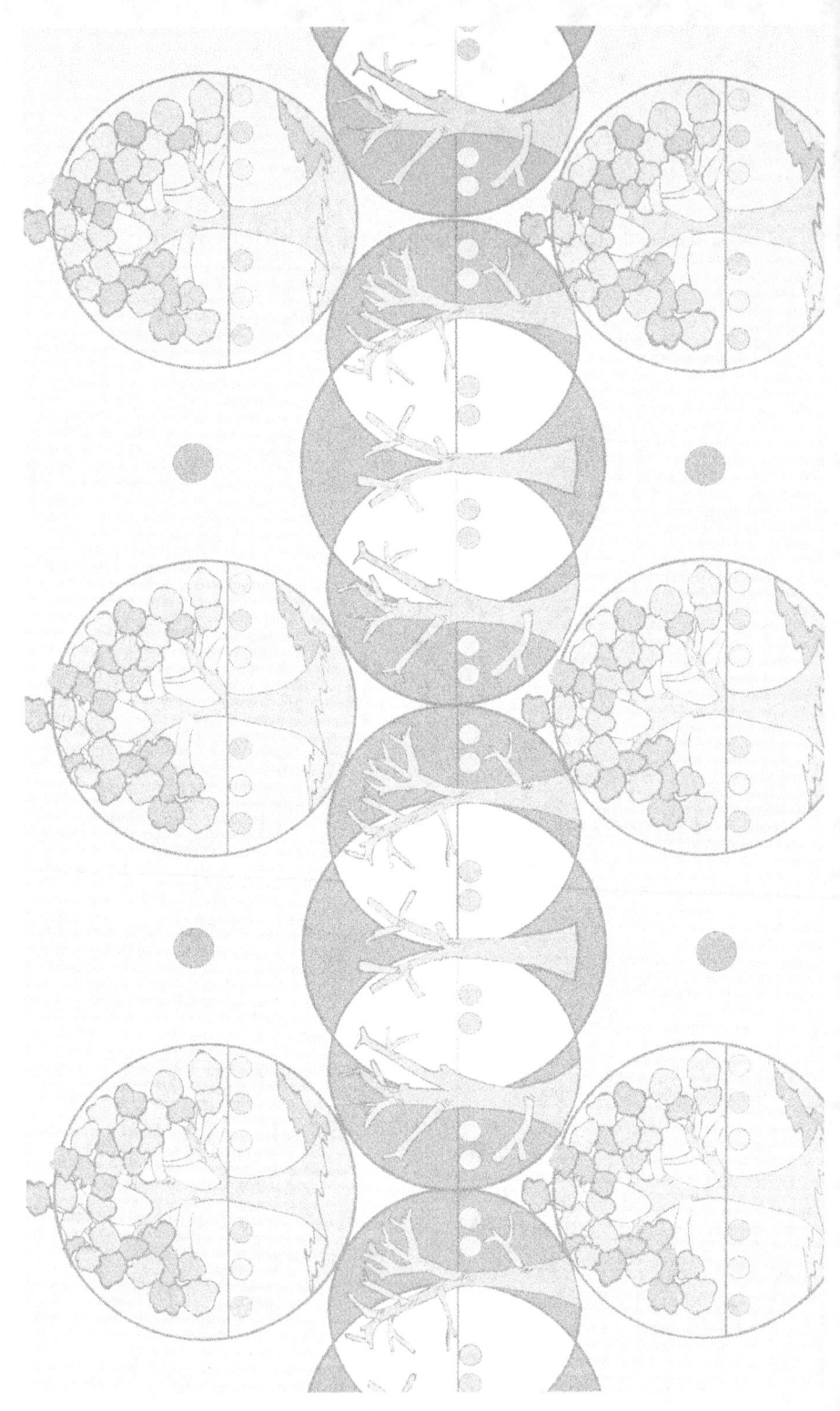